LIFE IN THE UN

D0496810

Passing the
Life in the UK Test

Official
Practice
Questions
and Answers

Published by TSO (The Stationery Office) and available from:

Online
www.tsoshop.co.uk

Mail, Telephone, Fax & E-mail
TSO
PO Box 29, Norwich, NR3 1GN
Telephone orders/General enquiries: 0870 600 5522
Fax orders: 0870 600 5533
E-mail: customer.services@tso.co.uk
Textphone 0870 240 3701

TSO@Blackwell and other Accredited Agents

Customers can also order publications from:
TSO Ireland
16 Arthur Street, Belfast BT1 4GD
Tel 028 9023 8451 Fax 028 9023 5401

First published 2009
Sixth impression May 2010

ISBN 978-0-11-341328-7

Designed and typeset by TSO

Printed in UK for The Stationery Office

P002362908 c100 5/10 3205

CONTENTS

INTRODUCTION

If you have decided that you would like to live in the UK permanently, or apply to become a British citizen, then you will need to pass the Life in the UK Test (unless you are exempt[1]).

The Life in the UK Test is based on the content of the main Home Office publication, *Life in the United Kingdom: A Journey to Citizenship*, published by The Stationery Office (TSO, 2007). **You should read this book very carefully** as it contains all the information you will need to know in order to answer the questions correctly in the Life in the UK Test.

If you need any further advice about the test (including how to prepare for it, how to tell if your English is good enough, and what happens after the test), then you should also read *Life in the United Kingdom: Official Citizenship Test Study Guide* (TSO, 2008).

The two books mentioned above are the only official publications which have been endorsed by the Home Office, and you should be wary of buying any other publications, as they may not provide the support that you need. Details of how to obtain the official publications are provided in the Related Publications section at the back of this book.

The purpose of the book you are reading now is to offer you as much practice as possible before you take your test. So as soon as you have studied the main Home Office publication, you can start testing your knowledge. This book contains 408 questions in total, arranged in 17 tests, each of 24 questions. Answers and helpful page references to the main publication are given at the end of each test, enabling you to see which pages you need to read again in the event of a wrong answer.

Although these practice questions are not the actual questions that you will get in the Life in the UK Test, by answering them correctly you can find out whether you are ready to take the test.

---

1   For a full list of exemptions, please refer to page 6 in the companion guide *Life in the United Kingdom: Official Citizenship Test Study Guide* (TSO, 2008).

About the test

The Life in the UK Test consists of 24 questions about aspects of life in Britain today. You take the test on a computer in an official test centre, and you are given 45 minutes to complete the test. Each person taking the test is given a different set of questions, so if you have to retake the test, you will be given a fresh set of questions. All the questions are based on Chapters 2, 3, 4, 5 and 6 of *Life in the United Kingdom: A Journey to Citizenship* (TSO, 2007).

In order to pass the test, you have to achieve a pass mark of around 75%.

How many types of question are there?

There are four types of question in the test. Each practice test in this book contains examples of each of these types of question, presented in random order.

The first type of question involves selecting one correct answer from four options. Here is an example of this type of question.

Where is the Prime Minister's official home in London?

- ☐ Downing Street
- ☐ Parliament Square
- ☐ Richmond Terrace
- ☐ Whitehall Place

(The correct answer is Downing Street.)

The second type of question involves deciding whether a statement is true or false. Here is an example of this second type of question.

Is the statement below TRUE or FALSE?

Citizens of the UK can vote in elections at the age of 18.

- ☐ TRUE
- ☐ FALSE

(The correct answer is TRUE.)

The third type of question involves selecting the statement which you think is correct from a choice of two statements. Here is an example of this third type of question.

Which of these statements is correct?

☐ Scottish bank notes are valid in all parts of the UK.
☐ Scottish bank notes are valid only in Scotland.

(The first statement is the correct answer.)

The final type of question involves selecting two correct answers from four options. You need to select **both** correct answers to get a point on this type of question. Here is an example of this fourth type of question.

Which TWO places can you go to if you need a National Insurance number?

☐ Department for Education and Skills
☐ Home Office
☐ Jobcentre Plus
☐ Social security office

(The correct answers are Jobcentre Plus and social security office.)

Practise taking the test

Before you take the test, you should aim to complete all the practice questions in this book. Complete one test at a time, and time yourself, allowing no more than 45 minutes per test. Note which questions you get wrong, and make sure you re-read the relevant pages in the main publication to ensure that your knowledge is sound.

When you go to the test centre to take the test, you can do a practice test of four questions before you start the actual test. You will have four minutes to do this practice test and you are allowed to take it twice before starting.

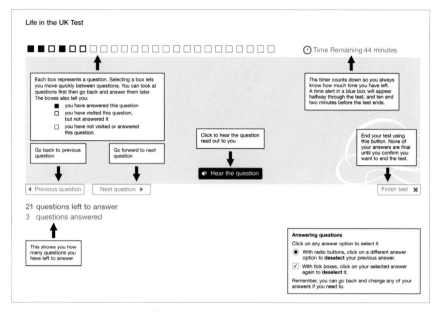

A navigation tutorial is available on the Life in the UK Test website (www.lifeintheuktest.gov.uk). This tutorial will help to familiarise you with the test layout.

Where can I find out more information about the test?

More information is provided in the companion book, *Life in the United Kingdom: Official Citizenship Test Study Guide* (TSO, 2008). Alternatively, you can contact the Life in the UK Test helpline on 0800 0154245 or go to the website www.lifeintheuktest.gov.uk

Good luck with your studying and with taking the test!

PRACTICE TEST 1

QUESTION 1   The official report of what happens in Parliament is called

☐ **A**   the constitution

☐ **B**   Hansard

☐ **C**   the Speaker's notes

☐ **D**   the monarchy

QUESTION 2   What percentage of the population of the UK live in England?

☐ **A**   65%

☐ **B**   72%

☐ **C**   76%

☐ **D**   84%

QUESTION 3   Which of these statements is correct?

☐ **A**   A debit card does not draw money from your bank account, but you will
           be sent a bill every month.

☐ **B**   A store card is like a credit card but can be used only in a particular shop.

QUESTION 4   In 2001, ethnic minority groups made up

☐ **A**   less than 5% of the population of England

☐ **B**   between 5 and 10% of the population of England

☐ **C**   between 10 and 15% of the population of England

☐ **D**   more than 15% of the population of England

QUESTION 5   In which TWO of the following places does the European Parliament meet?

☐ **A**   London

☐ **B**   Strasbourg

☐ **C**   Paris

☐ **D**   Brussels

QUESTION 6 Is the statement below   ☐ TRUE or ☐ FALSE?

'Your pay slip only shows how much money has been taken off for
  tax; it does not show National Insurance contributions.'

QUESTION 7 The proportion of young people who go on to higher education in the UK is

☐ **A**   1 in 2
☐ **B**   1 in 3
☐ **C**   1 in 4
☐ **D**   1 in 5

QUESTION 8 Is the statement below   ☐ TRUE or ☐ FALSE?

'Further education colleges only admit people up to the age of 19.'

QUESTION 9 In what year did Guy Fawkes attempt to plant a bomb in the
Houses of Parliament?

☐ **A**   1703
☐ **B**   1605
☐ **C**   1066
☐ **D**   1815

QUESTION 10 Which of the following statements is correct?

☐ **A**   The UK was a founder member of the European Economic Community.
☐ **B**   The UK was a founder member of the Council of Europe.

QUESTION 11 If you become unemployed, and are capable, available and trying to find
work, you may be able to claim

☐ **A**   an education support grant
☐ **B**   Jobseeker's Allowance
☐ **C**   an education maintenance allowance
☐ **D**   a state pension

QUESTION 12   How many women with children at school are in paid work?

☐ **A**   Nearly a quarter

☐ **B**   Nearly a half

☐ **C**   Nearly two-thirds

☐ **D**   Nearly three-quarters

QUESTION 13   Is the statement below   ☐ TRUE or ☐ FALSE?

'One person living in a flat or house is entitled to a 50% reduction in Council Tax.'

QUESTION 14   In England and Scotland, children take national tests when they are

☐ **A**   7, 9 and 11 years old

☐ **B**   5, 7 and 16 years old

☐ **C**   9, 14 and 16 years old

☐ **D**   7, 11 and 14 years old

QUESTION 15   Is the statement below   ☐ TRUE or ☐ FALSE?

'Britain does not have a written constitution.'

QUESTION 16   Some people speak with a Cockney accent in

☐ **A**   Birmingham

☐ **B**   Newcastle

☐ **C**   Glasgow

☐ **D**   London

QUESTION 17   Is the statement below   ☐ TRUE or ☐ FALSE?

'In the 16th and 18th centuries, the Huguenots left France and came to Britain because of famine.'

QUESTION 18   To drive a large lorry or bus in the UK, you must be aged at least

☐ **A**   17
☐ **B**   21
☐ **C**   18
☐ **D**   25

QUESTION 19   Is the statement below   ☐ TRUE or ☐ FALSE?

'The spiritual leader of the Church of England is the Archbishop of Canterbury.'

QUESTION 20   Which statement is correct?

☐ **A**   People in the UK are more likely to support a pressure group than join a political party.

☐ **B**   People in the UK are more likely to join a political party than support a pressure group.

QUESTION 21   Generally, the earliest legal age for children to do paid work is

☐ **A**   8
☐ **B**   10
☐ **C**   13
☐ **D**   14

QUESTION 22   Is the statement below   ☐ TRUE or ☐ FALSE?

'In the 1980s, the largest immigrant groups were from the West Indies, Ireland, India and Pakistan.'

QUESTION 23   Which TWO of the following documents prove your identity?

☐ **A**   A library card
☐ **B**   A pay slip
☐ **C**   A passport or travel document
☐ **D**   A provisional or full driving licence

QUESTION 24 Is the statement below ☐ TRUE or ☐ FALSE?

'There is no way to compare qualifications from abroad with those in the UK.'

Answers and pointers to questions in Practice Test 1

Question	Answer	Reference (page number in Life in the United Kingdom)	Notes
1	B	49	
2	D	35	
3	B	60	
4	B	37	In England, ethnic minority groups make up 9% of the total population.
5	B and D	53	
6	False	79	Pay slips should show both tax and NI contributions deducted.
7	B	31	
8	False	68	Most further education courses are free up to the age of 19 but further education colleges also offer courses for adults.
9	B	41	
10	B	52/53	The UK did not join the EEC until 1973, but was a founder member of the Council of Europe when it was created in 1949.
11	B	81	
12	D	29	
13	False	59	Single occupancy of a property entitles the occupant to a 25% reduction.
14	D	30	
15	True	43	The British constitution is not written down in any single document.
16	D	37	
17	False	27	In the 16th and 18th centuries, the Huguenots left France and came to Britain because of religious persecution.
18	B	71	

Question	Answer	Reference (page number in Life in the United Kingdom)	Notes
19	True	39	
20	A	47	
21	C	84	
22	False	28	In the 1980s, the largest immigrant groups were from the United States, Australia, South Africa and New Zealand.
23	C and D	73	
24	False	75	You can find out how qualifications compare at the National Academic Recognition Information Centre (NARIC).

PRACTICE TEST 2

QUESTION 1   Which statement is correct?

☐ **A**   Citizens of EU countries who live in the UK can vote in a general election.

☐ **B**   Citizens of the Commonwealth who live in the UK can vote in a general election.

QUESTION 2   Baptists are a type of

☐ **A**   Protestant Christian

☐ **B**   Roman Catholic

☐ **C**   Muslim

☐ **D**   Jew

QUESTION 3   Which TWO items could you provide as documentation when opening a bank or building society account?

☐ **A**   A current passport

☐ **B**   A signed photograph

☐ **C**   Your birth certificate

☐ **D**   Tenancy agreement or household bill showing your address

QUESTION 4   Which of the following statements is correct?

☐ **A**   The Geordie dialect is spoken in Tyneside.

☐ **B**   The Geordie dialect is spoken in Liverpool.

QUESTION 5   Elections in the UK have to be held at least every

☐ **A**   3 years

☐ **B**   4 years

☐ **C**   5 years

☐ **D**   6 years

QUESTION 6   Which of these statements is correct?

☐ **A**   You can apply for a National Insurance number by contacting HM Revenue and Customs.

☐ **B**   You can apply for a National Insurance number through Jobcentre Plus or your local social security office.

QUESTION 7   Is the statement below   ☐ TRUE or ☐ FALSE?

'Children often start part-time work when they are 11 years old.'

QUESTION 8   Which of these statements is correct?

☐ **A**   The National Curriculum covers English, maths and several other subjects but does not include modern foreign languages.

☐ **B**   The National Curriculum covers English, maths and several other subjects including modern foreign languages.

QUESTION 9   The 14th February celebrates

☐ **A**   Valentine's Day

☐ **B**   Guy Fawkes' night

☐ **C**   Hallowe'en

☐ **D**   Hogmanay

QUESTION 10   How many countries are there in the European Union?

☐ **A**   6

☐ **B**   15

☐ **C**   25

☐ **D**   27

QUESTION 11   Is the statement below   ☐ TRUE or ☐ FALSE?

'Adults who have been unemployed for six months are usually required to join New Deal if they wish to continue receiving benefit.'

QUESTION 12   The initials GCSE stand for

☐ **A**   Graduate Certificate of Secondary Education

☐ **B**   General Certificate of Special Education

☐ **C**   General Certificate of Secondary Education

☐ **D**   Grade Certificate of School Education

QUESTION 13   The National Health Service began in

☐ **A**   1921

☐ **B**   1945

☐ **C**   1948

☐ **D**   1972

QUESTION 14   Why did the Huguenots come to Britain?

☐ **A**   To invade the country and seize land

☐ **B**   To find jobs and a better life

☐ **C**   To avoid religious persecution

☐ **D**   To avoid a famine

QUESTION 15   Which statement is correct?

☐ **A**   The Prime Minister lives in Buckingham Palace.

☐ **B**   The Prime Minister lives at 10 Downing Street.

QUESTION 16   When you apply for a job, which person would NOT be suitable to ask for a reference?

☐ **A**   A family member

☐ **B**   A present employer

☐ **C**   A previous employer

☐ **D**   A college tutor

QUESTION 17   The patron saint of England is

- [ ] **A**   St David
- [ ] **B**   St George
- [ ] **C**   St Patrick
- [ ] **D**   St Andrew

QUESTION 18   Is the statement below   [ ] TRUE or [ ] FALSE?

'Taxis and cabs with no licence are not insured for fare-paying passengers and are not always safe.'

QUESTION 19   St Andrew's Day is celebrated in Scotland on the

- [ ] **A**   1st March
- [ ] **B**   23rd April
- [ ] **C**   30th November
- [ ] **D**   17th March

QUESTION 20   Is the statement below   [ ] TRUE or [ ] FALSE?

'Pressure groups cannot influence government policy.'

QUESTION 21   When you start a job, an employer should give you a written statement or contract within

- [ ] **A**   3 weeks
- [ ] **B**   1 month
- [ ] **C**   2 months
- [ ] **D**   3 months

QUESTION 22   Which of these statements is correct?

- [ ] **A**   The majority of young people take part in community events.
- [ ] **B**   A small number of young people take part in community events.

QUESTION 23   Is the statement below   ☐ TRUE or ☐ FALSE?

'Some primary and secondary schools in the UK are linked to the Church of England or Roman Catholic Church.'

QUESTION 24   What percentage of the UK population live in Wales?

☐ **A**   9%

☐ **B**   7%

☐ **C**   10%

☐ **D**   5%

Answers and pointers to questions in Practice Test 2

Question	Answer	Reference (page number in the *Life in the United Kingdom*)	Notes
1	B	49	EU citizens can vote in all elections except general elections.
2	A	39	
3	A and D	60	
4	A	37	Well-known dialects in England are Geordie (Tyneside), Scouse (Liverpool) and Cockney (London).
5	C	44	
6	B	80	
7	False	31	Children are not usually allowed to start work before they are 14 years old.
8	B	67	
9	A	40	
10	D	52	
11	False	82	You have to be unemployed for 18 months.
12	C	31	
13	C	62	It provides all residents with free health care and treatment.
14	C	27	In the 16th and 18th centuries, Huguenots came to Britain to escape religious persecution in France.
15	B	45	
16	A	76	
17	B	39	
18	True	71	To operate legally, all taxis and minicabs must have a licence and display a licence plate.
19	C	39	

Question	Answer	Reference (page number in Life in the United Kingdom)	Notes
20	False	47	Pressure and lobby groups try to influence government and play an important role in politics.
21	C	79	
22	A	33	
23	True	67	They are called 'faith schools'.
24	D	35	2.9 million people live in Wales.

PRACTICE TEST 3

QUESTION 1   When Parliament is sitting, Prime Minister's Questions happen

- ☐ **A**   every day
- ☐ **B**   twice a day
- ☐ **C**   once a week
- ☐ **D**   once a month

QUESTION 2   The number of bank holidays every year is

- ☐ **A**   2
- ☐ **B**   3
- ☐ **C**   4
- ☐ **D**   5

QUESTION 3   Is the statement below   ☐ TRUE or ☐ FALSE?

'Credit unions are financial co-operatives owned and controlled by their members. Interest rates in credit unions are usually higher than in banks and building societies.'

QUESTION 4   Which of these statements is correct?

- ☐ **A**   45% of all ethnic minority people live in London.
- ☐ **B**   55% of all ethnic minority people live in London.

QUESTION 5   Is the following statement   ☐ TRUE or ☐ FALSE?

'The UK has a written constitution.'

QUESTION 6   The government department responsible for collecting taxes is

- ☐ **A**   the Department for Work and Pensions
- ☐ **B**   the Home Office
- ☐ **C**   HM Revenue and Customs
- ☐ **D**   the Central Office of Information

QUESTION 7   Which TWO examinations do young people take at 16?

    ☐ **A**   GCSE

    ☐ **B**   AGCE

    ☐ **C**   SQA standard grade

    ☐ **D**   SQA higher grade

QUESTION 8   Young people from families with low income can get financial help with their studies when they leave school at 16. This help is called

    ☐ **A**   education support grant

    ☐ **B**   further learning and training support allowance

    ☐ **C**   education maintenance allowance

    ☐ **D**   post-16 education allowance

QUESTION 9   The population of Scotland is just over

    ☐ **A**   1 million

    ☐ **B**   3 million

    ☐ **C**   5 million

    ☐ **D**   7 million

QUESTION 10   Which of the following statements is correct?

    ☐ **A**   Civil servants have to be members of the political party of the government they serve.

    ☐ **B**   Civil servants have to be politically neutral and professional.

QUESTION 11   Advice and information on setting up your own business is available from

    ☐ **A**   job centres

    ☐ **B**   solicitors

    ☐ **C**   Business Link

    ☐ **D**   your local library

QUESTION 12   What proportion of the population of Britain have used illegal drugs at one time?

☐ **A**   About a tenth

☐ **B**   About a quarter

☐ **C**   About a third

☐ **D**   About a half

QUESTION 13   In the UK, electricity is supplied at

☐ **A**   90 volts

☐ **B**   220 volts

☐ **C**   240 volts

☐ **D**   360 volts

QUESTION 14   Which of these statements is correct?

☐ **A**   In the 1950s, centres were set up in the West Indies to recruit bus drivers for the UK.

☐ **B**   In the 1950s, centres were set up in India and Pakistan to recruit bus drivers for the UK.

QUESTION 15   The Chancellor of the Exchequer is responsible for

☐ **A**   education

☐ **B**   health

☐ **C**   the economy

☐ **D**   legal affairs

QUESTION 16   Is the statement below   ☐ TRUE or ☐ FALSE?

'You should not ask questions in an interview.'

QUESTION 17 Which of these statements is correct?

☐ **A** In Wales, children take national tests in education when they are 7, 11 and 14 years old.

☐ **B** In Wales, children take a national test in education when they are 14 years old.

QUESTION 18 Is the statement below ☐ TRUE or ☐ FALSE?

'The landlord of a pub may allow people aged 14 to come into the pub but they are not allowed to drink alcohol.'

QUESTION 19 Which TWO are Christian religious groups?

☐ **A** Roman Catholic

☐ **B** Buddhist

☐ **C** Sikh

☐ **D** Baptists

QUESTION 20 Which TWO statements about the Speaker of the House of Commons are true?

☐ **A** The Speaker keeps order during debates in the House of Commons.

☐ **B** The Speaker represents the king or queen in the House of Commons.

☐ **C** The Speaker is elected by MPs of the Opposition.

☐ **D** The Speaker is politically neutral.

QUESTION 21 Which statement is correct?

☐ **A** A pay slip shows how much money you have paid in tax and National Insurance contributions.

☐ **B** A pay slip shows how much money you have paid in tax but does not show National Insurance contributions.

QUESTION 22 Is the statement below ☐ TRUE or ☐ FALSE?

'Smoking is generally not allowed in public places.'

QUESTION 23   Which TWO of the following statements are true?

☐ **A**   A baby must be registered within 6 weeks of birth.

☐ **B**   If the parents are not married, only the father can register the birth.

☐ **C**   If the parents are not married, only the mother can register the birth.

☐ **D**   A baby must be registered by the age of 1.

QUESTION 24   Is the following statement   ☐ TRUE or ☐ FALSE?

'The population of the North West of England has increased in recent years.'

Answers and pointers to questions in Practice Test 3

Question	Answer	Reference (page number in Life in the United Kingdom)	Notes
1	C	46	
2	C	39	There are four bank holidays and four other public holidays a year.
3	False	61	Interest rates in credit unions are usually lower than in banks and building societies.
4	A	37	
5	False	41	The British constitution is not written down.
6	C	79	
7	A and C	31	
8	C	68	
9	C	35	The population of Scotland was 5.1 million in 2005.
10	B	47	
11	C	82	
12	C	32	
13	C	58	
14	A	27	
15	C	45	
16	False	76	If you ask questions, it shows you are interested.
17	B	30	In Wales, teachers assess children's progress when they are 7 and 11, but they do not take a national test until they are 14.
18	True	70	
19	A and D	39	
20	A and D	46	The Speaker is elected by fellow MPs to keep order during debates and make sure rules are followed.
21	A	79	

Question	Answer	Reference (page number in Life in the United Kingdom)	Notes
22	True	31	
23	A and C	65	
24	False	35	Although the general population of the UK has increased in the last 20 years, in some areas such as the North East and North West of England there has been a decline.

PRACTICE TEST 4

QUESTION 1 Which statement is correct?

☐ **A** Most of the money for local authority services comes from the government through taxes.

☐ **B** Most of the money for local authority services comes from Council Tax.

QUESTION 2 Is the statement below ☐ TRUE or ☐ FALSE?

'A census takes place in the UK every five years.'

QUESTION 3 Which of these statements is correct?

☐ **A** Jobcentre Plus offices have information only for jobseekers.

☐ **B** Jobcentre Plus offices have information for jobseekers and can provide information on welfare benefits.

QUESTION 4 St Andrew is the patron saint of which country?

☐ **A** England

☐ **B** Scotland

☐ **C** Wales

☐ **D** Northern Ireland

QUESTION 5 Which of the following countries is NOT a member of the Commonwealth?

☐ **A** Mozambique

☐ **B** Seychelles

☐ **C** Singapore

☐ **D** Indonesia

QUESTION 6 If you are self-employed, you are responsible for paying which TWO of the following?

☐ **A** NI contributions

☐ **B** NHS contributions

☐ **C** State retirement pension contributions

☐ **D** Your own tax

QUESTION 7   A 'gap year' describes

- ☐ **A**   the school summer holidays
- ☐ **B**   a year that students spend working in industry
- ☐ **C**   a year between school and university which students spend travelling or working
- ☐ **D**   the year after GCSEs

QUESTION 8   Is the statement below   ☐ TRUE or ☐ FALSE?

'To drink alcohol in a pub you must be aged 16 or over.'

QUESTION 9   Which of the following statements is correct?

- ☐ **A**   Information in the census is immediately available for the public to search.
- ☐ **B**   Information in the census is kept secret for 100 years.

QUESTION 10   Is the following statement   ☐ TRUE or ☐ FALSE?

'The Welsh Assembly is responsible for taxation in Wales.'

QUESTION 11   Which of these statements is correct?

- ☐ **A**   Women who are expecting a baby are entitled to at least 16 weeks' maternity leave.
- ☐ **B**   Women who are expecting a baby are entitled to at least 26 weeks' maternity leave.

QUESTION 12   Is the statement below   ☐ TRUE or ☐ FALSE?

'Half of all young people in the UK have taken part in fundraising or collecting money for charity.'

QUESTION 13   You must register the birth of a baby within

☐ **A**   24 hours of the birth

☐ **B**   a week of the birth

☐ **C**   a month of the birth

☐ **D**   6 weeks of the birth

QUESTION 14   Is the statement below   ☐ TRUE or ☐ FALSE?

*'After the Second World War, the British government invited people
from Ireland and other parts of Europe to come to the UK.'*

QUESTION 15   Which statement is correct?

☐ **A**   The Welsh Assembly Government is in Cardiff.

☐ **B**   The Welsh Assembly Government is in Swansea.

QUESTION 16   Which statement is correct?

☐ **A**   A letter of application is a short letter attached to an application form.

☐ **B**   A covering letter is a short letter attached to an application form.

QUESTION 17   Is the statement below   ☐ TRUE or ☐ FALSE?

'It is illegal to be drunk in a public place.'

QUESTION 18   Which statement is correct?

☐ **A**   After the age of 70, drivers must renew their licence every 3 years.

☐ **B**   After the age of 70, drivers must renew their licence every 5 years.

QUESTION 19   Is the statement below   ☐ TRUE or ☐ FALSE?

'There are more people aged 60 and over than children under 16.'

QUESTION 20   Is the statement below   ☐ TRUE or ☐ FALSE?

*'The Cabinet makes important decisions about government policy.
The policy often needs to be approved by Parliament.'*

QUESTION 21   Which TWO places give you information about maternity and paternity leave?

☐ **A**   Your personnel department at work
☐ **B**   The post office
☐ **C**   Your local GP
☐ **D**   The Citizens' Advice Bureau

QUESTION 22   Since 1979 the number of refugees from South East Asia who have been allowed to settle in the UK is

☐ **A**   less than 2,500
☐ **B**   between 2,501 and 10,000
☐ **C**   between 10,001 and 25,000
☐ **D**   more than 25,000

QUESTION 23   Which of the following statements is correct?

☐ **A**   The National Trust is a charity that works to preserve important buildings in the UK.
☐ **B**   The National Trust is a government-run organisation that safeguards the pensions of top civil servants.

QUESTION 24   Which of these statements is correct?

☐ **A**   In the UK, about 10% of the population regularly goes to a religious service.
☐ **B**   In the UK, about 20% of the population regularly goes to a religious service.

Answers and pointers to questions in Practice Test 4

Question	Answer	Reference (page number in Life in the United Kingdom)	Notes
1	A	48	Only about 20% of the money comes from Council Tax.
2	False	36	A census has been taken every ten years since 1801, except in 1941.
3	B	61	
4	B	39	St Andrew is the patron saint of Scotland.
5	D	52	
6	A and D	82	
7	C	31	
8	False	70	You must be 18 to drink alcohol in a pub. At 16 you can drink wine or beer with a meal in a hotel or restaurant.
9	B	36	Census information remains confidential and anonymous; it can only be released to the public after 100 years.
10	False	47	Policy and laws governing defence, foreign affairs, taxation and social security remain under central government control.
11	B	84	
12	True	33	
13	D	65	
14	True	27	
15	A	47	Cardiff is the capital of Wales.
16	B	76	A letter of application is longer and gives more details about why you are applying for the job.
17	True	32	
18	A	71	

Question	Answer	Reference (page number in Life in the United Kingdom)	Notes
19	True	35	
20	True	46	
21	A and D	84	Trade union representatives also give information on these subjects.
22	D	28	
23	A	70	
24	A	38	Many people have religious beliefs but only 10% go to a religious service.

PRACTICE TEST 5

QUESTION 1   Is the statement below   ☐ TRUE or ☐ FALSE?

'European law is legally binding in the UK.'

QUESTION 2   Which of these statements is correct?

☐ **A**   In Scotland, some people in the Highlands and Islands speak Gaelic.

☐ **B**   In Scotland, some people in the south speak Gaelic.

QUESTION 3   Where do you register a birth?

☐ **A**   At the hospital where the birth took place

☐ **B**   At your GP's practice

☐ **C**   At the Register Office

☐ **D**   By calling NHS Direct

QUESTION 4   The percentage of the population who attend religious services in the UK is

☐ **A**   5%

☐ **B**   10%

☐ **C**   15%

☐ **D**   20%

QUESTION 5   Is the following statement   ☐ TRUE or ☐ FALSE?

'The Government cannot instruct the police what to do in any particular case.'

QUESTION 6   Hogmanay is a traditional celebration in

☐ **A**   Scotland

☐ **B**   England

☐ **C**   Wales

☐ **D**   Northern Ireland

QUESTION 7 Young people are eligible for Jobseeker's Allowance at the age of

- ☐ **A** 18
- ☐ **B** 16
- ☐ **C** 17
- ☐ **D** 15

QUESTION 8 Is the statement below   ☐ TRUE or ☐ FALSE?

'Everyone who has paid enough National Insurance contributions
will get a state pension when they retire.'

QUESTION 9 The percentage of people in the UK in 2001 who said they were Muslims was

- ☐ **A** 1.6%
- ☐ **B** 2.7%
- ☐ **C** 3.4%
- ☐ **D** 4.2%

QUESTION 10 How many seats does the UK hold in the European Parliament?

- ☐ **A** 58
- ☐ **B** 68
- ☐ **C** 78
- ☐ **D** 88

QUESTION 11 Fathers who have worked for their employer for at least 26 weeks are entitled to how much paternity leave?

- ☐ **A** 1 week
- ☐ **B** 3 weeks
- ☐ **C** 8 days
- ☐ **D** 2 weeks

QUESTION 12 In the 2001 general election, how many first-time voters used their vote?

☐ **A** 1 in 4

☐ **B** 1 in 5

☐ **C** 1 in 10

☐ **D** 1 in 3

QUESTION 13 Is the statement below   ☐ TRUE or ☐ FALSE?

'You can attend a hospital without a GP's letter only if it is an emergency.'

QUESTION 14 When did the British government encourage people from Ireland and Europe to come to the UK to work?

☐ **A** After the Second World War

☐ **B** After the First World War

☐ **C** In the late 1960s

☐ **D** In the 1980s

QUESTION 15 The devolved administrations in Wales and Scotland can make decisions on which TWO matters?

☐ **A** Defence

☐ **B** Transport

☐ **C** Education

☐ **D** Foreign policy

QUESTION 16 Is the statement below   ☐ TRUE or ☐ FALSE?

'In certain jobs, an employer may ask for a criminal record check.'

QUESTION 17 Which TWO part-time jobs are the most common for children?

☐ **A** Delivering newspapers

☐ **B** Working in supermarkets or newsagents

☐ **C** Delivering post

☐ **D** Cleaning

QUESTION 18   Is the statement below   ☐ TRUE or ☐ FALSE?

'People over 65 years of age can apply for a free television licence.'

QUESTION 19   Is the statement below   ☐ TRUE or ☐ FALSE?

'Everyone in the UK has the legal right to practise a religion.'

QUESTION 20   The Whips are a small group of MPs responsible for which TWO things?

☐ **A**   Calling general elections

☐ **B**   Representing the government at the opening of Parliament

☐ **C**   Making sure MPs vote in the House of Commons

☐ **D**   Discipline in their party

QUESTION 21   Which statement is correct?

☐ **A**   Maternity leave depends on how long a woman has been working for her employer.

☐ **B**   Maternity pay depends on how long a woman has been working for her employer.

QUESTION 22   Is the statement below   ☐ TRUE or ☐ FALSE?

'It is common for employers to ask women to leave their jobs when they marry.'

QUESTION 23   Is the statement below   ☐ TRUE or ☐ FALSE?

'The Department of Work and Pensions provides guidance on who is allowed to work in the UK.'

QUESTION 24   What is the age requirement for someone wishing to see a PG classification film, video or DVD?

☐ **A**   Suitable for all ages, but some parts may be unsuitable for children so parents should decide

☐ **B**   Suitable for children aged 8 years and over if accompanied by an adult

☐ **C**   Children under 15 years of age are not allowed to see or rent the film

☐ **D**   Suitable for unaccompanied children aged 8 years and over

Answers and pointers to questions in Practice Test 5

Question	Answer	Reference (page number in Life in the United Kingdom)	Notes
1	True	53	
2	A	37	
3	C	65	
4	B	38	
5	True	49	The police have operational independence which means that the government cannot instruct them what to do in any particular case.
6	A	40	It is celebrated on 31st December.
7	A	81	
8	True	80	
9	B	38	
10	C	44	
11	D	84	
12	B	33	
13	True	62	
14	A	27	
15	B and C	47	The UK government is responsible for defence and foreign policy.
16	True	76	
17	A and B	31	
18	False	70	People over 75 years of age can apply for a free television licence.
19	True	38	
20	C and D	44	
21	B	84	
22	False	29	Employers are not allowed to do this.
23	False	75	The Home Office provides guidance on work eligibility.
24	A	69	

PRACTICE TEST 6

QUESTION 1 Which statement is correct?

☐ **A** A judge decides if someone is guilty of a serious crime.

☐ **B** A jury decides if someone is guilty of a serious crime.

QUESTION 2 What percentage of the population of Scotland is made up of people from ethnic minority groups?

☐ **A** 9%

☐ **B** 2%

☐ **C** 5%

☐ **D** Less than 1%

QUESTION 3 Which of the following TWO types of people get their prescriptions free of charge?

☐ **A** People aged 60 or over

☐ **B** People under 18 years of age

☐ **C** Pregnant women or those with a baby under 12 months old

☐ **D** People on the minimum wage

QUESTION 4 Is the following statement ☐ TRUE or ☐ FALSE?

'In the UK, 1st April is a day when people play jokes on each other.'

QUESTION 5 Which of the following countries does NOT operate a system of proportional representation?

☐ **A** England

☐ **B** Wales

☐ **C** Scotland

☐ **D** Northern Ireland

QUESTION 6   The state pension age is

☐ **A**   65 years for men and 60 for women

☐ **B**   70 years for men and 65 for women

☐ **C**   67 years for men and 62 for women

☐ **D**   72 years for men and 65 for women

QUESTION 7   Is this statement   ☐ TRUE or ☐ FALSE?

'There is a strong link between the use of hard drugs and mental illness.'

QUESTION 8   Which of these statements is correct?

☐ **A**   A TV licence covers all TV equipment at one address, even if people rent different rooms at that address.

☐ **B**   A TV licence covers all TV equipment at one address, but people who rent different rooms at that address must each buy a separate licence.

QUESTION 9   Which of the following statements is correct?

☐ **A**   Fireworks are traditionally set off on 31st October in the UK.

☐ **B**   Fireworks are traditionally set off on 5th November in the UK.

QUESTION 10   The present voting age of 18 in the UK was set in

☐ **A**   1966

☐ **B**   1969

☐ **C**   1973

☐ **D**   1960

QUESTION 11   Is the statement below   ☐ TRUE or ☐ FALSE?

'Any child under school-leaving age (16) seeking to do paid work must apply for a licence from the local authority.'

QUESTION 12   AS levels are gained by completing

- ☐ **A**   three AS units
- ☐ **B**   four AS units
- ☐ **C**   three GCSEs
- ☐ **D**   four GCSEs

QUESTION 13   Which statement is correct?

- ☐ **A**   In the UK, most women have babies in hospital.
- ☐ **B**   In the UK, most women have babies at home.

QUESTION 14   Is the statement below   ☐ TRUE or ☐ FALSE?

'In most households, men have the main responsibility for childcare and housework.'

QUESTION 15   Which statement is correct?

- ☐ **A**   There are a small number of jobs where the discrimination laws do not apply.
- ☐ **B**   Discrimination laws apply to all jobs.

QUESTION 16   Is the statement below   ☐ TRUE or ☐ FALSE?

'A Prime Minister usually resigns when their party loses a general election.'

QUESTION 17   Which of these statements is correct?

- ☐ **A**   In the 1950s, Britain encouraged people from the West Indies to come to the UK to drive buses.
- ☐ **B**   In the 1950s, Britain encouraged people from the West Indies to come to the UK to work in factories.

QUESTION 18   Which statement is correct?

☐ **A**   When you are learning to drive, you can drive a car with someone who is aged 21 and over and has had a full licence for more than a year.

☐ **B**   When you are learning to drive, you can drive a car with someone who is aged 21 and over and has had a full licence for more than 3 years.

QUESTION 19   Valentine's Day is on

☐ **A**   1st March

☐ **B**   23rd April

☐ **C**   30th November

☐ **D**   14th February

QUESTION 20   When was the Scottish Parliament formed?

☐ **A**   1972

☐ **B**   1979

☐ **C**   1999

☐ **D**   2001

QUESTION 21   Which statement is correct?

☐ **A**   Most employees who are aged 16 or over, get 4 weeks' paid holiday a year.

☐ **B**   Most employees who are aged 16 or over, get 6 weeks' paid holiday a year.

QUESTION 22   In the 1840s, many Irish men came to Britain and did which TWO things?

☐ **A**   Worked in shops

☐ **B**   Built railways

☐ **C**   Built canals

☐ **D**   Worked in mines

QUESTION 23 Which TWO of the following types of people can act as your referee in support of a job application?

☐ **A** A family member

☐ **B** Your current or previous employer

☐ **C** Your college tutor

☐ **D** A personal friend

QUESTION 24 A census has been taken every 10 years since 1801, except during

☐ **A** the First World War

☐ **B** the Second World War

☐ **C** the Falklands War

☐ **D** the Boer War

Answers and pointers to questions in Practice Test 6

Question	Answer	Reference (page number in Life in the United Kingdom)	Notes
1	B	48	A judge decides on the penalty if someone is guilty of a serious crime.
2	B	37	Ethnic minorities form 2% of the Scottish population.
3	A and C	63	
4	True	40	
5	A	44 and 47	In England MPs are elected in a system called 'first past the post' where the candidate who gets the most votes is elected and the government is formed by the party which wins the majority of the constituencies.
6	A	80	
7	True	32	
8	B	70	
9	B	41	
10	B	49	
11	True	84	
12	A	31	
13	A	64	
14	False	29	In most households, women continue to have the main responsibility for childcare and housework.
15	A	77	
16	True	45	
17	A	27	
18	B	71	
19	D	40	It is a day when lovers send cards and gifts.

Question	Answer	Reference (page number in Life in the United Kingdom)	Notes
20	C	47	The Scottish Parliament was formed in 1999 and is in Edinburgh, the capital of Scotland.
21	A	79	This includes national holidays.
22	B and C	27	
23	B and C	76	Personal friends and family members are not usually acceptable as referees.
24	B	36	

PRACTICE TEST 7

QUESTION 1   Which of the following statements is correct?

☐ **A**   Civil servants have to politically neutral.

☐ **B**   Civil servants have to be politically aligned to the elected government.

QUESTION 2   The Grand National is a

☐ **A**   tennis tournament

☐ **B**   golf championship

☐ **C**   football match

☐ **D**   horse race

QUESTION 3   Is the statement below   ☐ TRUE or ☐ FALSE?

'All patients registering with a GP are entitled to a free health check.'

QUESTION 4   When will the next census be taken?

☐ **A**   2010

☐ **B**   2011

☐ **C**   2012

☐ **D**   2013

QUESTION 5   Is the following statement   ☐ TRUE or ☐ FALSE?

'Members of the public may not attend debates in the Houses of Parliament.'

QUESTION 6   Which of these statements is correct?

☐ **A**   You need a National Insurance number when you start work.

☐ **B**   You don't need a National Insurance number when you start work.

QUESTION 7   Is the statement below   ☐ TRUE or ☐ FALSE?

'There are UK teams for rugby and football.'

QUESTION 8   Which people are not allowed into betting shops or gambling clubs?

☐ **A**   People aged under 16

☐ **B**   People aged under 17

☐ **C**   People aged under 18

☐ **D**   People aged under 21

QUESTION 9   Is the following statement   ☐ TRUE or ☐ FALSE?

'At school, children learn about customs and traditions such as
Eid ul-Fitr, Diwali and Hanukkah from various religions.'

QUESTION 10   Is the following statement   ☐ TRUE or ☐ FALSE?

'People who rent properties do not have to pay Council Tax.'

QUESTION 11   Children under 16 are not allowed to work

☐ **A**   before 6 am or after 6 pm

☐ **B**   before 9 am or after 5 pm

☐ **C**   before 8 am or after 6 pm

☐ **D**   before 7 am or after 7 pm

QUESTION 12   Is the statement below   ☐ TRUE or ☐ FALSE?

'Women make up 45% of the workforce.'

QUESTION 13   Which statement is correct?

☐ **A**   You register a birth at the Register Office.

☐ **B**   You register a birth with the local council.

QUESTION 14   Women in Britain first got the vote in

☐ **A**   1882

☐ **B**   1918

☐ **C**   1928

☐ **D**   1945

QUESTION 15   Which TWO responsibilities does an MP have?

☐ **A**   To debate national issues

☐ **B**   To help create new laws

☐ **C**   To represent the UK in the European Parliament

☐ **D**   To choose the Home Secretary

QUESTION 16   Is the statement below   ☐ TRUE or ☐ FALSE?

'The majority of laws protecting people at work apply to part-time and full-time jobs.'

QUESTION 17   Women could vote at the same age as men in

☐ **A**   1914

☐ **B**   1919

☐ **C**   1928

☐ **D**   1945

QUESTION 18   Is the statement below   ☐ TRUE or ☐ FALSE?

'Housing associations are independent not-for-profit organisations which provide housing for rent.'

QUESTION 19   The number of children and young people up to the age of 19 in the UK is

☐ **A**   13 million

☐ **B**   14 million

☐ **C**   15 million

☐ **D**   16 million

QUESTION 20   Is the statement below   ☐ TRUE or ☐ FALSE?

'By law, the radio and television must give equal time to opposing political parties at election time.'

QUESTION 21   Tax which is taken from people's earnings is paid directly to

☐ **A**   Department for Trade and Industry

☐ **B**   your trade union

☐ **C**   your local authority

☐ **D**   HM Revenue and Customs

QUESTION 22   Which of these statements is correct?

☐ **A**   In the 1950s, many industries advertised for workers from overseas.

☐ **B**   In the 1980s, many industries advertised for workers from overseas.

QUESTION 23   Which of these statements is correct?

☐ **A**   The Home Office provides guidance on the applicability of overseas qualifications.

☐ **B**   The National Academic Recognition Information Centre (NARIC) provides guidance on the applicability of overseas qualifications.

QUESTION 24   Is the statement below   ☐ TRUE or ☐ FALSE?

'The Church of England is a Catholic church and has existed since the 1530s.'

Answers and pointers to questions in Practice Test 7

Question	Answer	Reference (page number in Life in the United Kingdom)	Notes
1	A	47	
2	D	41	
3	True	62	
4	B	36	
5	False	50	The public can listen to debates in the Palace of Westminster from public galleries both in the House of Commons and in the House of Lords.
6	A	80	
7	False	41	England, Scotland, Wales and Northern Ireland have their own teams.
8	C	70	
9	True	40	
10	False	48	Council Tax applies to all domestic properties whether owned or rented.
11	D	84	
12	True	29	
13	A	65	
14	B	29	In 1918, women aged over 30 were given the right to vote. In 1928, women won the right to vote at 21, the same age as men.
15	A and B	44	Members of the European Parliament (MEPs) represent the UK in the European Parliament. The Prime Minister chooses the Home Secretary.
16	True	77	
17	C	29	
18	True	56	
19	C	30	

Question	Answer	Reference (page number in Life in the United Kingdom)	Notes
20	True	49	At election time, radio and television coverage has to be balanced.
21	D	79	
22	A	27	
23	B	75	
24	False	39	The Church of England is a Protestant church and has existed since the 1530s.

PRACTICE TEST 8

QUESTION 1   Is the statement below   ☐ TRUE or ☐ FALSE?

'People who buy their own homes usually pay for it with a mortgage, which is a loan from a bank or building society usually paid back over 15 years.'

QUESTION 2   On Remembrance Day, people wear

☐ **A**   a daffodil
☐ **B**   a red poppy
☐ **C**   a red rose
☐ **D**   a white rose

QUESTION 3   In which TWO places can you find the name of a dentist?

☐ **A**   By enquiring at your GP's practice
☐ **B**   By calling NHS Direct
☐ **C**   By enquiring at a Citizens' Advice Bureau
☐ **D**   By calling your local authority

QUESTION 4   Is the following statement   ☐ TRUE or ☐ FALSE?

'The monarch of the UK is not allowed to marry anyone who is not Protestant.'

QUESTION 5   A quango is

☐ **A**   a government department
☐ **B**   a non-departmental public body
☐ **C**   an arm of the judiciary
☐ **D**   an educational establishment

QUESTION 6   It is against the law for employers to discriminate against someone on the basis of which TWO factors from the list below?

☐ **A**   Weight
☐ **B**   Religion
☐ **C**   Height
☐ **D**   Sex

QUESTION 7   A 'suffragette' was

- ☐ **A**   a woman who suffered persecution
- ☐ **B**   a woman who demonstrated for greater rights
- ☐ **C**   a woman who worked during the First World War
- ☐ **D**   a woman who stayed at home to raise her family

QUESTION 8   Is the statement below   ☐ TRUE or ☐ FALSE?

'It is a criminal offence to have a car without proper motor insurance and it is also illegal to allow someone to use your car if they are not insured to drive it.'

QUESTION 9   The percentage of Black or Black British people in the UK in 2001 was

- ☐ **A**   2%
- ☐ **B**   4%
- ☐ **C**   5%
- ☐ **D**   7%

QUESTION 10   Is the following statement   ☐ TRUE or ☐ FALSE?

'All members of both Houses of Parliament are democratically elected.'

QUESTION 11   Which of these statements is correct?

- ☐ **A**   Children aged 13–16 years cannot work for more than 12 hours in any school week.
- ☐ **B**   Children aged 13–16 years cannot work for more than 10 hours in any school week.

QUESTION 12   In the UK, the number of children and young people under 19 years old is

- ☐ **A**   13 million
- ☐ **B**   15 million
- ☐ **C**   17 million
- ☐ **D**   19 million

QUESTION 13 Which statement is correct?

☐ **A** People aged under 16 are not allowed to buy a lottery ticket or scratch card.

☐ **B** People aged under 18 are not allowed to buy a lottery ticket or scratch card.

QUESTION 14 Is the statement below ☐ TRUE or ☐ FALSE?

'In the UK, it is illegal to discriminate against women at work because of their sex.'

QUESTION 15 Is the statement below ☐ TRUE or ☐ FALSE?

'The civil service is politically neutral.'

QUESTION 16 National Insurance (NI) contributions are used to pay for which TWO benefits?

☐ **A** National Health Service

☐ **B** Jobseeker's Allowance

☐ **C** Education maintenance allowance

☐ **D** State retirement pension

QUESTION 17 Which of these statements is correct?

☐ **A** On average, women are paid 20% less than men.

☐ **B** On average, women are paid 30% less than men.

QUESTION 18 Which statement is correct?

☐ **A** The film classification U means that it is suitable for everyone.

☐ **B** The film classification U means that it is suitable for anyone over the age of 4.

QUESTION 19   The most senior person in the Church of Scotland is the

- ☐ **A**   Moderator
- ☐ **B**   monarch
- ☐ **C**   Archbishop of Canterbury
- ☐ **D**   Prime Minister

QUESTION 20   Parliament is made up of which TWO of the following?

- ☐ **A**   The House of Lords
- ☐ **B**   The Cabinet
- ☐ **C**   The monarchy
- ☐ **D**   The House of Commons

QUESTION 21   Which service does income tax NOT pay for?

- ☐ **A**   Roads
- ☐ **B**   Rubbish collection
- ☐ **C**   Education
- ☐ **D**   Police

QUESTION 22   Is the statement below   ☐ TRUE or ☐ FALSE?

   'On average, boys leave school with better qualifications than girls.'

QUESTION 23   Choose TWO places from the list below where jobs are advertised.

- ☐ **A**   Local library
- ☐ **B**   Local job centre
- ☐ **C**   Post office
- ☐ **D**   Local and national newspapers

QUESTION 24   In 2001, how many people said they were Christian?

☐ **A**   4 out of 10

☐ **B**   5 out of 10

☐ **C**   7 out of 10

☐ **D**   9 out of 10

Answers and pointers to questions in Practice Test 8

Question	Answer	Reference (page number in Life in the United Kingdom)	Notes
1	False	55	The loan is normally paid back over 25 years.
2	B	41	People wear red poppies to remember those who died in wars.
3	B and C	64	
4	True	39	
5	B	49	
6	B and D	77	
7	B	29	In the late 19th and early 20th centuries, an increasing number of women campaigned and demonstrated for greater rights, and in particular the right to vote. They became known as 'suffragettes'.
8	True	72	
9	A	36	In the 2001 census, there were 1% Black Caribbean, 0.8% Black African and 0.2% Black Other people (1% + 0.8% + 0.2% = 2%)
10	False	45	Members of the House of Lords are not elected. They either inherit their place in the House of Lords, are senior judges or bishops of the Church of England, or are life peers appointed by a Prime Minister.
11	A	84	
12	B	30	
13	A	70	
14	True	29	During the 1960s and 1970s, Parliament passed new laws giving women the right to equal pay and prohibiting employers from discriminating against women because of their sex.
15	True	47	
16	A and D	80	

Question	Answer	Reference (page number in Life in the United Kingdom)	Notes
17	A	29	
18	B	69	
19	A	39	
20	A and D	43	
21	B	79	
22	False	29	On average, girls leave school with better qualifications than boys.
23	B and D	75	
24	C	38	

PRACTICE TEST 9

QUESTION 1   Why should you use a solicitor when buying a property?

☐ **A**   They check that the property is structurally sound.

☐ **B**   They carry out legal checks on the property, the seller and the local area.

☐ **C**   They negotiate the repayment terms of your mortgage with the bank or building society.

☐ **D**   They act on behalf of both buyer and seller.

QUESTION 2   Which of these statements is correct?

☐ **A**   Many people from Liverpool speak with a Scouse dialect.

☐ **B**   Many people from Tyneside speak with a Scouse dialect.

QUESTION 3   Which of these statements is correct?

☐ **A**   If you want to see a doctor, you should call NHS Direct on 0845 46 47.

☐ **B**   If you want to see a doctor, you should make an appointment at your GP's surgery or visit an NHS walk-in centre.

QUESTION 4   The 31st October celebrates

☐ **A**   Valentine's Day

☐ **B**   Guy Fawkes' night

☐ **C**   Hallowe'en

☐ **D**   Hogmanay

QUESTION 5   Is the statement below   ☐ TRUE or ☐ FALSE?

'Citizens of an EU member state have the right to travel and work in any EU country.'

QUESTION 6   Is the statement below   ☐ TRUE or ☐ FALSE?

'Your employer can dismiss you for being a trade union member.'

QUESTION 7   In the UK, children must attend school until they are

- [ ] **A**   14 years old
- [ ] **B**   15 years old
- [ ] **C**   16 years old
- [ ] **D**   17 years old

QUESTION 8   You must have a current MOT (Ministry of Transport) certificate for your car if it is more than

- [ ] **A**   2 years old
- [ ] **B**   3 years old
- [ ] **C**   4 years old
- [ ] **D**   5 years old

QUESTION 9   Gaelic is spoken in which TWO countries in the UK?

- [ ] **A**   England
- [ ] **B**   Wales
- [ ] **C**   Scotland
- [ ] **D**   Northern Ireland

QUESTION 10   The aims of the United Nations are

- [ ] **A**   to function as a single market
- [ ] **B**   to prevent war and promote peace and security
- [ ] **C**   to examine decisions made by the European Union
- [ ] **D**   to promote democracy, good government and eradicate poverty

QUESTION 11   Which TWO jobs from the following list are children aged under 16 not allowed to do?

- [ ] **A**   Sell alcohol, cigarettes or medicines
- [ ] **B**   Deliver newspapers
- [ ] **C**   Work in a kitchen
- [ ] **D**   Casual gardening

QUESTION 12   Young people can vote in a general election at the age of

- ☐ **A**   16
- ☐ **B**   17
- ☐ **C**   18
- ☐ **D**   21

QUESTION 13   Is the statement below   ☐ TRUE or ☐ FALSE?

'All dogs in public places must wear a collar showing the name and address of their owner.'

QUESTION 14   From which TWO places were people invited to come and work in the UK during the 1950s?

- ☐ **A**   India
- ☐ **B**   New Zealand
- ☐ **C**   Russia
- ☐ **D**   West Indies

QUESTION 15   Which statement is correct?

- ☐ **A**   The Queen is the heir to the throne.
- ☐ **B**   Prince Charles is the heir to the throne.

QUESTION 16   Is the statement below   ☐ TRUE or ☐ FALSE?

'Volunteering gives you useful experience that may help you get a job.'

QUESTION 17   Which of these statements is correct?

- ☐ **A**   At school, children learn only about Christian festivals.
- ☐ **B**   At school, children learn about customs and traditions from all religions.

QUESTION 18   Is the statement below   ☐ TRUE or ☐ FALSE?

'A home-school agreement states all the things that both the school and parents should do to ensure that the child gets a good education.'

QUESTION 19   Is the statement below   ☐ TRUE or ☐ FALSE?

'Most people in the UK live in towns and cities.'

QUESTION 20   Which TWO countries are members of the Commonwealth?

☐ **A**   Indonesia

☐ **B**   Malaysia

☐ **C**   Pakistan

☐ **D**   Ireland

QUESTION 21   Which statement is correct?

☐ **A**   Children aged between 13 and 16 years old can work up to 2 hours on a Sunday.

☐ **B**   Children aged between 13 and 16 years old can work up to 4 hours on a Sunday.

QUESTION 22   Which of these statements is correct?

☐ **A**   A gap year is the time a parent stays at home to look after a baby or small child.

☐ **B**   A gap year is a year between school and university which students spend travelling or working.

QUESTION 23   Many job applications will require a covering letter and

☐ **A**   a document showing proof of identity

☐ **B**   your National Insurance number

☐ **C**   a curriculum vitae

☐ **D**   a signed photograph

QUESTION 24   Is the statement below   ☐ TRUE or ☐ FALSE?

'In the 1980s, the largest immigrant groups were from South East Asia.'

Answers and pointers to questions in Practice Test 9

Question	Answer	Reference (page number in Life in the United Kingdom)	Notes
1	B	56	
2	A	37	People from Tyneside speak with a Geordie accent.
3	B	63	
4	C	41	
5	True	52	
6	False	81	
7	C	30	
8	B	72	
9	C and D	37	
10	B	53	The UK is one of the five permanent members of the UN.
11	A and C	84	
12	C	33	
13	True	70	
14	A and D	27/28	
15	B	44	
16	True	76	
17	B	40	
18	True	68	
19	True	37	
20	B and C	52	
21	A	84	
22	B	31	
23	C	76	
24	False	28	In the 1980s, the largest immigrant groups were from the United States, Australia, South Africa and New Zealand.

PRACTICE TEST 10

QUESTION 1   Which of these statements is correct?

☐ **A**   When renting a property, a deposit is paid to the landlord at the beginning of the tenancy to cover the cost of any damage.

☐ **B**   When renting a property, a deposit is paid to the landlord at the beginning of the tenancy to cover his/her administrative costs.

QUESTION 2   St David is the patron saint of

☐ **A**   England

☐ **B**   Scotland

☐ **C**   Wales

☐ **D**   Northern Ireland

QUESTION 3   You can receive health advice and treatment when you are pregnant and after you have had the baby from which TWO sources?

☐ **A**   Your GP

☐ **B**   The Family Planning Association

☐ **C**   Your health visitor

☐ **D**   The local nursery

QUESTION 4   Is the following statement   ☐ TRUE or ☐ FALSE?

'The UK football team is very important to British people.'

QUESTION 5   Which TWO of the following are members of the Cabinet?

☐ **A**   The Chancellor of the Exchequer

☐ **B**   The Speaker of the House of Commons

☐ **C**   The Leader of the Opposition

☐ **D**   The Home Secretary

QUESTION 6   Where can you find details of trade unions in the UK?

☐ **A**   The Home Office

☐ **B**   Your local library

☐ **C**   Trades Union Congress (TUC website)

☐ **D**   Jobcentre Plus website

QUESTION 7   In the 1950s, textile and engineering firms sent agents to which TWO countries to find workers?

☐ **A**   Russia

☐ **B**   India

☐ **C**   Vietnam

☐ **D**   Pakistan

QUESTION 8   Which of these statements is correct?

☐ **A**   For cars and motorcycles the speed limit on single carriageways is 60 mph.

☐ **B**   For cars and motorcycles the speed limit on single carriageways is 70 mph.

QUESTION 9   Is the following statement   ☐ TRUE or ☐ FALSE?

'Every household in the UK is required by law to complete a census form.'

QUESTION 10   The group of senior MPs appointed by the Leader of the Opposition to lead the criticism of government ministers is called

☐ **A**   the Opposition Cabinet

☐ **B**   the Shadow ministers

☐ **C**   the Shadow Cabinet

☐ **D**   the Opposition ministers

QUESTION 11   Is the statement below   ☐ TRUE or ☐ FALSE?

'There is no national minimum wage for those aged under 16.'

QUESTION 12 Is the statement below   ☐ TRUE or ☐ FALSE?

'School-age boys smoke more than girls.'

QUESTION 13 When you obtain a mortgage to buy a house, who normally carries out checks on the property to ensure that it is sound?

☐ **A** A solicitor

☐ **B** A plumber

☐ **C** A surveyor

☐ **D** An electrician

QUESTION 14 Is the statement below   ☐ TRUE or ☐ FALSE?

'Women have had equal voting rights with men in the UK since 1928.'

QUESTION 15 Who opens Parliament each year?

☐ **A** The Archbishop of Canterbury

☐ **B** The Prime Minister

☐ **C** The Speaker of the House of Commons

☐ **D** The Queen

QUESTION 16 Which TWO places can you contact about getting a National Insurance number?

☐ **A** The Home Office

☐ **B** The Department for Work and Pensions

☐ **C** Jobcentre Plus

☐ **D** Your local social security office

QUESTION 17 The minimum wage for 18–21-year-olds is

☐ **A** £5.35 per hour

☐ **B** £4.35 per hour

☐ **C** £3.30 per hour

☐ **D** £4.45 per hour

QUESTION 18   How many days a year must schools be open?

☐ **A**   160
☐ **B**   180
☐ **C**   190
☐ **D**   210

QUESTION 19   After Christianity, which are the TWO largest religious groups in the UK?

☐ **A**   Jewish
☐ **B**   Muslim
☐ **C**   Hindu
☐ **D**   Buddhist

QUESTION 20   Which TWO statements about the Commonwealth are true?

☐ **A**   The Prime Minister is head of the Commonwealth.
☐ **B**   There are 53 members.
☐ **C**   Membership is for countries that were part of the British Empire.
☐ **D**   The Commonwealth has no power over its members.

QUESTION 21   Maternity leave is

☐ **A**   6 weeks
☐ **B**   12 weeks
☐ **C**   26 weeks
☐ **D**   36 weeks

QUESTION 22   In the 1950s, workers came from Bangladesh and India to work in which TWO industries?

☐ **A**   Mining
☐ **B**   Farming
☐ **C**   Textiles
☐ **D**   Engineering

QUESTION 23   Is the statement below   ☐ TRUE or ☐ FALSE?

'If you are applying for a job which involves working with vulnerable people, it will be necessary for your employer to do a CRB (Criminal Records Bureau) check.'

QUESTION 24   How much has the population of the UK grown since 1971?

☐ **A**   6.1%
☐ **B**   7.5%
☐ **C**   8.6%
☐ **D**   7.7%

Answers and pointers to questions in Practice Test 10

Question	Answer	Reference (page number in Life in the United Kingdom)	Notes
1	A	57	
2	C	39	St David's Day is celebrated on 1st March.
3	A and C	65	
4	False	41	There are no UK teams for football and rugby. England, Scotland, Wales and Northern Ireland have their own teams.
5	A and D	45	
6	C	81	
7	B and D	28	
8	A	72	
9	True	36	
10	C	46	
11	True	85	
12	False	31	School-age girls smoke more than boys.
13	C	56	A surveyor will usually make a report on behalf of the bank or building society that is providing you with the mortgage.
14	True	29	In 1918, women aged over 30 were given the right to vote. In 1928, women won the right to vote at 21, the same age as men.
15	D	44	
16	C and D	80	
17	D	79	
18	C	68	Term dates are decided by the governing body or the local education authority.
19	B and C	38	

Question	Answer	Reference (page number in Life in the United Kingdom)	Notes
20	B and D	52	The Queen is head of the Commonwealth and membership is voluntary.
21	C	84	
22	C and D	27	
23	True	76	
24	D	35	

PRACTICE TEST 11

QUESTION 1   Approximately what proportion of people in the UK own their own home?

☐ **A**   One-third

☐ **B**   One-quarter

☐ **C**   One-half

☐ **D**   Two-thirds

QUESTION 2   Is the statement below   ☐ TRUE or ☐ FALSE?

'The information in a census is available to the public after 10 years.'

QUESTION 3   Is the statement below   ☐ TRUE or ☐ FALSE?

'Educational assessment in the UK is based on key stage tests at ages 7, 11 and 14.'

QUESTION 4   The Notting Hill Carnival is held in

☐ **A**   Liverpool

☐ **B**   Manchester

☐ **C**   Edinburgh

☐ **D**   London

QUESTION 5   How many parliamentary constituencies are there?

☐ **A**   464

☐ **B**   564

☐ **C**   646

☐ **D**   664

QUESTION 6   If you are worried about health and safety at your workplace, you should

☐ **A**   make a report to the police

☐ **B**   write to the Department of Work and Pensions

☐ **C**   talk to your supervisor, manager or trade union representative

☐ **D**   contact a solicitor

QUESTION 7   Is the statement below   ☐ TRUE or ☐ FALSE?

> *'The number of people migrating to Britain from the West Indies, India, Pakistan and Bangladesh increased during the late 1960s and early 1970s.'*

QUESTION 8   To drive a car or motorcycle in the UK you must be at least

☐ **A**   15 years old
☐ **B**   16 years old
☐ **C**   17 years old
☐ **D**   18 years old

QUESTION 9   Is the following statement   ☐ TRUE or ☐ FALSE?

> *'More people attend religious services in England and Wales than in Scotland and Northern Ireland.'*

QUESTION 10   Life peers are appointed by

☐ **A**   the monarch
☐ **B**   the Prime Minister
☐ **C**   the Speaker of the House of Commons
☐ **D**   the Chief Whip

QUESTION 11   Is the statement below   ☐ TRUE or ☐ FALSE?

> *'The minimum wage is the same for all workers.'*

QUESTION 12   Which of these statements is correct?

☐ **A**   Smoking is not allowed in public buildings.
☐ **B**   Smoking is allowed at work places if the majority of workers smoke.

QUESTION 13   Is the statement below   ☐ TRUE or ☐ FALSE?

> *'When you rent a property, you have to pay the landlord a deposit at the beginning of the tenancy to cover the cost of administration.'*

QUESTION 14   In which year did married women get the right to divorce their husband?

- ☐ **A**   1837
- ☐ **B**   1857
- ☐ **C**   1875
- ☐ **D**   1882

QUESTION 15   Which statement is correct?

- ☐ **A**   The public elects members of the House of Lords.
- ☐ **B**   The public does not elect members of the House of Lords.

QUESTION 16   Is the statement below   ☐ TRUE or ☐ FALSE?

'It is legal to carry a small amount of cannabis.'

QUESTION 17   Which statement is correct?

- ☐ **A**   Trade unions are organisations that try to improve the trade between two countries.
- ☐ **B**   Trade unions are organisations that try to improve the pay and conditions of their members.

QUESTION 18   Is the statement below   ☐ TRUE or ☐ FALSE?

'A television licence covers all the TV equipment in one house but people who rent different rooms at the same address need to buy a separate licence.'

QUESTION 19   Is the statement below   ☐ TRUE or ☐ FALSE?

'The monarch is not allowed to marry anyone of the Roman Catholic faith.'

QUESTION 20   Which TWO of the following can make decisions about UK government policy?

- ☐ **A**   The Cabinet
- ☐ **B**   Lobby groups
- ☐ **C**   The monarch
- ☐ **D**   The Prime Minister

QUESTION 21 Which statement is correct?

☐ **A** Children under 16 are not allowed to work in a kitchen but can deliver milk.

☐ **B** Children under 16 are not allowed to work in a kitchen or deliver milk.

QUESTION 22 Is the statement below ☐ TRUE or ☐ FALSE?

'Most children live with both their parents.'

QUESTION 23 Information about training opportunities can be found from which TWO of the following?

☐ **A** The local library
☐ **B** The local council offices
☐ **C** Learndirect
☐ **D** The Home Office

QUESTION 24 Is the following statement ☐ TRUE or ☐ FALSE?

'The Scottish Parliament can pass legislation for Scotland on all matters.'

Answers and pointers to questions in Practice Test 11

Question	Answer	Reference (page number in Life in the United Kingdom)	Notes
1	D	55	
2	False	36	It is released to the public after 100 years.
3	False	67	Educational assessment is carried out in England and Northern Ireland at the ages of 7, 11 and 14. In Wales, testing only takes place at 14, and in Scotland, teachers test children when they are ready.
4	D	40	The Notting Hill Carnival is held in west London.
5	C	44	
6	C	80	
7	False	28	The number of people migrating from these areas fell in the late 1960s and early 1970s because the government passed new laws to restrict immigration to Britain.
8	C	71	
9	False	38	
10	A	45	Life peers are appointed by the Queen on the advice of the Prime Minister.
11	False	79	It depends on your age.
12	A	31	
13	False	57	The deposit covers the cost of any damage. It is usually equal to one month's rent.
14	B	29	Until 1857, a married woman had no right to divorce her husband.
15	B	45	Members of the House of Lords are not elected and do not represent a constituency.
16	False	32	It is illegal to possess cannabis.
17	B	81	
18	True	70	

Question	Answer	Reference (page number in Life in the United Kingdom)	Notes
19	True	39	
20	A and D	43	
21	B	84	
22	True	30	
23	A and C	76	
24	False	47	Certain matters are reserved for the UK Parliament.

PRACTICE TEST 12

QUESTION 1   Is the statement below   ☐ TRUE or ☐ FALSE?

'If you apply for council housing, you will be assessed according to need using a system of points. You get more points if you are homeless, have children, or are chronically ill.'

QUESTION 2   The population of England is about

☐ **A**   40 million
☐ **B**   50 million
☐ **C**   60 million
☐ **D**   70 million

QUESTION 3   Who is responsible for making sure a child goes to school?

☐ **A**   The local education authority
☐ **B**   The headteacher of the school
☐ **C**   The parent or guardian of the child
☐ **D**   The local councillor

QUESTION 4   Is the following statement   ☐ TRUE or ☐ FALSE?

'Ulster Scots is a dialect which is spoken in Northern Ireland.'

QUESTION 5   Is the following statement   ☐ TRUE or ☐ FALSE?

'Discipline in the parliamentary parties is carried out by a group of people called the Whips.'

QUESTION 6   Which of these statements is correct?

☐ **A**   Trade unions are organisations that aim to improve the pay and working conditions of their members.
☐ **B**   Trade unions are organisations that organise social events for their members.

QUESTION 7   Is the statement below   ☐ TRUE or ☐ FALSE?

'At work, it is an employee's responsibility to follow safety regulations.'

QUESTION 8   St Patrick's Day is celebrated on

☐ **A**   1st March

☐ **B**   17th March

☐ **C**   23rd April

☐ **D**   30th November

QUESTION 9   Is the statement below   ☐ TRUE or ☐ FALSE?

'Driving away after an accident without stopping is a criminal offence.'

QUESTION 10   In order to vote in an election you must have

☐ **A**   a UK passport

☐ **B**   your name on the electoral register

☐ **C**   an identity card

☐ **D**   a place to live

QUESTION 11   If you have qualifications from another country, whom should you contact to see how they compare with UK qualifications?

☐ **A**   Local job centre

☐ **B**   The National Academic Recognition Information Centre

☐ **C**   The National Work Permit Office

☐ **D**   The International Qualifications Board

QUESTION 12   In the 1970s, the UK accepted large numbers of refugees from which TWO places?

☐ **A**   Uganda

☐ **B**   South Africa

☐ **C**   South East Asia

☐ **D**   Soviet Union

QUESTION 13   If you are homeless or have problems with a landlord, you can get help at which TWO of the following places?

- ☐ **A**   Shelter
- ☐ **B**   The Citizens' Advice Bureau
- ☐ **C**   The government
- ☐ **D**   The police

QUESTION 14   Jewish people came to Britain from Poland, Ukraine and Belarus to escape racist attacks

- ☐ **A**   from 1830 to 1850
- ☐ **B**   from 1880 to 1910
- ☐ **C**   from 1910 to 1920
- ☐ **D**   from 1930 to 1945

QUESTION 15   The Lord Chancellor is responsible for

- ☐ **A**   the economy
- ☐ **B**   legal affairs
- ☐ **C**   health
- ☐ **D**   transport

QUESTION 16   If you think that you have lost your job unfairly, you can take your case to an employment tribunal. You usually have to do this within

- ☐ **A**   21 days
- ☐ **B**   1 month
- ☐ **C**   3 months
- ☐ **D**   6 months

QUESTION 17   Which of these statements is correct?

☐ **A**   The women who campaigned for more rights for women were called suffragettes.

☐ **B**   The women who campaigned for more rights for women were called Huguenots.

QUESTION 18   If you have a driving licence from outside the European Union, you can drive in the UK for

☐ **A**   up to 6 months

☐ **B**   up to 12 months

☐ **C**   up to 2 years

☐ **D**   up to 10 years

QUESTION 19   In English schools, how many stages is the curriculum divided into?

☐ **A**   5

☐ **B**   4

☐ **C**   3

☐ **D**   6

QUESTION 20   Is the statement below   ☐ TRUE or ☐ FALSE?

'The UN aims to prevent war and to promote international peace and security.'

QUESTION 21   Is the statement below   ☐ TRUE or ☐ FALSE?

'An employer can be prosecuted for illegally employing a child.'

QUESTION 22   Which of these statements is correct?

☐ **A**   AGCE is the new name for an AS level.

☐ **B**   AGCE is the new name for an A level.

QUESTION 23 Which of these statements is correct?

☐ **A** If you are sexually harassed at work, you should tell a friend, colleague or trade union representative and ask the person harassing you to stop.

☐ **B** If you are sexually harassed at work, you should inform the police immediately.

QUESTION 24 The heir to the throne is

☐ **A** Princess Anne

☐ **B** Prince Charles

☐ **C** Prince Philip

☐ **D** Prince William

Answers and pointers to questions in Practice Test 12

Question	Answer	Reference (page number in Life in the United Kingdom)	Notes
1	True	56	
2	B	35	The population of England is about 50 million. The total UK population is about 60 million.
3	C	66	
4	True	37	
5	True	44	
6	A	81	
7	True	80	Employers have a legal duty to make sure a workplace is safe, but it is up to the employee to make sure they follow safety regulations.
8	B	39	St Patrick's Day is celebrated in Northern Ireland on 17th March.
9	True	72	
10	B	49	
11	B	75	
12	A and C	28	
13	A and B	57	
14	B	27	From 1880 to 1910, a large number of Jewish people came to Britain to escape racist attacks (called 'pogroms') in what was then called the Russian Empire.
15	B	45	
16	C	81	
17	A	29	
18	B	72	
19	B	67	

Question	Answer	Reference (page number in Life in the United Kingdom)	Notes
20	True	53	
21	True	85	
22	B	31	
23	A	78	
24	B	44	Prince Charles, the Queen's oldest son, is the heir to the throne.

PRACTICE TEST 13

QUESTION 1   How are water rates billed?

☐ **A**   They are included in your Council Tax.

☐ **B**   They are billed either as one payment (lump sum) or a series of instalments.

QUESTION 2   Is the statement below   ☐ TRUE or ☐ FALSE?

'In the UK, the birth rate and the death rate are declining.'

QUESTION 3   At what age do children in Scotland start secondary school?

☐ **A**   10

☐ **B**   12

☐ **C**   13

☐ **D**   14

QUESTION 4   Which TWO of these are names for the Church of England?

☐ **A**   Methodist

☐ **B**   Episcopal

☐ **C**   Anglican

☐ **D**   Presbyterian

QUESTION 5   Which TWO of the following can vote in all UK public elections?

☐ **A**   Citizens of the Irish Republic resident in the UK

☐ **B**   Citizens of EU states resident in the UK

☐ **C**   Citizens of the Commonwealth resident in the UK

☐ **D**   Anyone resident in the UK

QUESTION 6 From which TWO places can you obtain advice if you have a problem at work and need to take further action?

- ☐ **A** Citizens' Advice Bureau
- ☐ **B** Your local MP
- ☐ **C** Your employer
- ☐ **D** The national Advisory, Conciliation and Arbitration Service (ACAS)

QUESTION 7 By what percentage is the average hourly pay of women lower than men's?

- ☐ **A** 5%
- ☐ **B** 10%
- ☐ **C** 15%
- ☐ **D** 20%

QUESTION 8 Which of these statements is correct?

- ☐ **A** To open a bank account, you will need to provide proof of identity, such as a passport or National Insurance number card, and a document showing your name and current address, such as a recent utilities bill.
- ☐ **B** To open a bank account, you will need to provide a document showing your name and current address, such as a recent utilities bill.

QUESTION 9 On Christmas Day, people in the UK usually

- ☐ **A** stay at home and eat a special meal
- ☐ **B** spend the day fasting
- ☐ **C** go to work
- ☐ **D** go shopping

QUESTION 10 Is the following statement ☐ TRUE or ☐ FALSE?

'The Government can control what is written in newspapers in the UK.'

QUESTION 11 Is the statement below ☐ TRUE or ☐ FALSE?

'A parent or carer may be prosecuted if they do not ensure that their child receives a proper education.'

QUESTION 12 Which of these statements is correct?

- ☐ **A** A woman had no right to divorce her husband until 1927.
- ☐ **B** A woman had no right to divorce her husband until 1857.

QUESTION 13 Who is responsible for the rubbish collection?

- ☐ **A** The government
- ☐ **B** The local authority
- ☐ **C** The owner of the property
- ☐ **D** The housing association

QUESTION 14 The Irish famine was in the middle of the

- ☐ **A** 1820s
- ☐ **B** 1830s
- ☐ **C** 1840s
- ☐ **D** 1850s

QUESTION 15 Which statement is correct?

- ☐ **A** The police service is organised locally.
- ☐ **B** The police service is organised nationally.

QUESTION 16 Is the statement below   ☐ TRUE or ☐ FALSE?

'Employers are responsible for the behaviour of their employees while they are at work.'

QUESTION 17 How many children live with only one parent?

- ☐ **A** Nearly a third
- ☐ **B** Nearly a half
- ☐ **C** Nearly two-thirds
- ☐ **D** Nearly a quarter

QUESTION 18 Is the statement below ☐ TRUE or ☐ FALSE?

'When they leave school, young people from families with low income can get an education maintenance allowance to help with their studies.'

QUESTION 19 Which of these statements is correct?

☐ **A** There is a link between the Church of Scotland and the state.

☐ **B** There is a link between the Church of England and the state.

QUESTION 20 The Council of Europe makes conventions and charters on which of the following TWO areas?

☐ **A** Transport

☐ **B** Taxes

☐ **C** Human rights and democracy

☐ **D** Education

QUESTION 21 Which statement is correct?

☐ **A** Redundancy pay depends on the length of time you were employed.

☐ **B** Redundancy pay depends on the amount of money you were paid.

QUESTION 22 Is the following statement ☐ TRUE or ☐ FALSE?

'About a quarter of the population have used illegal drugs at one time or another.'

QUESTION 23 Advice and information on racial discrimination, sex discrimination and disability issues can be obtained from

☐ **A** your local job centre

☐ **B** the Commission for Equality and Human Rights

☐ **C** the Department for Work and Pensions

☐ **D** your local library

QUESTION 24   Which TWO of the following constitute Parliament?

☐ **A**   The House of Commons

☐ **B**   The Cabinet

☐ **C**   The House of Lords

☐ **D**   The civil service

Answers and pointers to questions in Practice Test 13

Question	Answer	Reference (page number in Life in the United Kingdom)	Notes
1	B	58	
2	True	35	
3	B	66	
4	B and C	39	The Church of England is called the Anglican Church in other countries and the Episcopal Church in Scotland.
5	A and C	49	All UK-born and naturalised citizens have the right to vote in all public elections, as do citizens of the Commonwealth and the Irish Republic if resident in the UK.
6	A and D	81	
7	D	29	
8	A	73	
9	A	40	
10	False	49	The UK has a free press which means that what is written in newspapers is free of government control.
11	True	85	
12	B	29	
13	B	58	
14	C	27	In the mid-1840s, there was a terrible famine in Ireland and many people migrated to Britain.
15	A	49	
16	True	78	
17	D	30	
18	True	68	
19	B	39	The Church of Scotland is not controlled by the state.

Question	Answer	Reference (page number in Life in the United Kingdom)	Notes
20	C and D	53	The Council of Europe does not make laws but does draw up charters and conventions.
21	A	81	
22	False	32	About a third of the population have used illegal drugs.
23	B	78	
24	A and C	43	

PRACTICE TEST 14

QUESTION 1   Which of these statements is correct?

☐ **A**   The amount of Council Tax you pay is reduced if you work for your local council.

☐ **B**   The amount of Council Tax you pay depends on the size and value of your property.

QUESTION 2   The 5th November is

☐ **A**   Valentine's Day

☐ **B**   Hogmanay

☐ **C**   Remembrance Day

☐ **D**   Guy Fawkes' night

QUESTION 3   Which of these statements is correct?

☐ **A**   Education at state schools in the UK is free and this includes the cost of school uniform and sports wear.

☐ **B**   Education at state schools in the UK is free but parents have to pay for school uniform and sports wear.

QUESTION 4   When do people in the UK wear poppies?

☐ **A**   New Year's Day

☐ **B**   Valentine's Day

☐ **C**   Remembrance Day

☐ **D**   Mother's Day

QUESTION 5   The initials MEP stand for

☐ **A**   Member Elected to Parliament

☐ **B**   Member of the Edinburgh Parliament

☐ **C**   Member of the European Parliament

☐ **D**   Member of the Executive Parliament

QUESTION 6   For which TWO reasons from the list below can an employer give you a warning?

- ☐ **A**   You are overweight
- ☐ **B**   You are unacceptably late for work
- ☐ **C**   You cannot do your job properly
- ☐ **D**   You are the wrong sex

QUESTION 7   What percentage of children live with only one parent?

- ☐ **A**   13%
- ☐ **B**   18%
- ☐ **C**   22%
- ☐ **D**   25%

QUESTION 8   Is the statement below   ☐ TRUE or ☐ FALSE?

'NHS Direct is a 24-hour telephone service which gives information on health conditions.'

QUESTION 9   The Scouse dialect is spoken in

- ☐ **A**   London
- ☐ **B**   Liverpool
- ☐ **C**   Tyneside
- ☐ **D**   Wales

QUESTION 10   Which statement is correct?

- ☐ **A**   The governing body of the EU is the Council of the European Union.
- ☐ **B**   The governing body of the EU is the Council of Europe.

QUESTION 11   Which statement is correct?

- ☐ **A**   The Home Office gives guidance on who is allowed to work in the UK.
- ☐ **B**   The Department for Work and Pensions gives guidance on who is allowed to work in the UK.

QUESTION 12 Is the statement below   ☐ TRUE or ☐ FALSE?

'There are more men than women at university.'

QUESTION 13 Which TWO groups of people from the following have to pay for their prescriptions?

☐ **A** Pregnant women or those with a baby under 12 months old

☐ **B** People who work for the NHS

☐ **C** People aged 60 or over

☐ **D** People who get housing benefit

QUESTION 14 Is the statement below   ☐ TRUE or ☐ FALSE?

'In the late 1960s the government passed new laws which restricted immigration from Australia, New Zealand and Canada.'

QUESTION 15 Is the statement below   ☐ TRUE or ☐ FALSE?

'Everyone who lives in the UK has the right to vote and do jury service.'

QUESTION 16 Which government-funded project provides advice to self-employed people?

☐ **A** Business Link

☐ **B** New Deal

☐ **C** Start Up for New Businesses

☐ **D** The National Self-employed Helpline

QUESTION 17 Is the statement below   ☐ TRUE or ☐ FALSE?

'In the 1950s, there was a shortage of jobs in the UK.'

QUESTION 18 The speed limit on single carriageways is

☐ **A** 30 mph

☐ **B** 50 mph

☐ **C** 60 mph

☐ **D** 70 mph

QUESTION 19 Which TWO are public holidays?

☐ **A** Boxing Day

☐ **B** St George's Day

☐ **C** 1st January

☐ **D** Hallowe'en

QUESTION 20 Is the statement below ☐ TRUE or ☐ FALSE?

'Members of the House of Lords are elected democratically.'

QUESTION 21 Which statement is correct?

☐ **A** Discrimination laws do not apply if the job involves working for someone in their own home.

☐ **B** Discrimination laws apply to all jobs in the UK, with no exceptions.

QUESTION 22 In education, how many AS (Advanced Subsidiary) units make up an AGCE (Advanced General Certificate of Education)?

☐ **A** 3

☐ **B** 6

☐ **C** 4

☐ **D** 8

QUESTION 23 Is the statement below ☐ TRUE or ☐ FALSE?

'The minimum wage in the UK for workers aged 22 and above is £5.35 an hour.'

QUESTION 24 Is the following statement ☐ TRUE or ☐ FALSE?

'The monarch of the UK makes decisions on government policies.'

Answers and pointers to questions in Practice Test 14

Question	Answer	Reference (page number in Life in the United Kingdom)	Notes
1	B	59	
2	D	41	People set off fireworks at home or go to firework displays.
3	B	66	
4	C	41	Many people wear poppies on Remembrance Day in memory of those who died fighting in the First World War.
5	C	45	
6	B and C	81	
7	D	30	
8	True	63	
9	B	37	
10	A	52	
11	A	75	
12	False	29	There are more women than men at university.
13	B and D	63	
14	False	28	In the late 1960s and early 1970s, the government passed new laws to restrict immigration to Britain although immigrants from 'old' Commonwealth countries such as Australia, New Zealand and Canada did not have to face such strict controls.
15	False	49	Only UK-born and naturalised citizens over the age of 18 can vote and do jury service.
16	A	82	
17	False	27	There was a shortage of labour in the UK.
18	C	72	
19	A and C	40	Boxing Day is the 26th December.

Question	Answer	Reference (page number in Life in the United Kingdom)	Notes
20	False	45	Members of the House of Lords are not elected.
21	A	77	
22	B	31	
23	True	79	
24	False	43	The King or Queen does not rule the country but appoints the government and the decisions on government policies are made by the Prime Minister and Cabinet.

PRACTICE TEST 15

QUESTION 1   Who is responsible for the collection and disposal of waste?

- ☐ **A**   The owner of the property
- ☐ **B**   The residents' association
- ☐ **C**   The local authority
- ☐ **D**   The government

QUESTION 2   The census collects information on which TWO topics?

- ☐ **A**   Marital status
- ☐ **B**   Hobbies
- ☐ **C**   Height
- ☐ **D**   Occupation

QUESTION 3   What TWO types of schools are there in the UK in addition to state schools?

- ☐ **A**   Holy schools
- ☐ **B**   Independent schools
- ☐ **C**   Tertiary schools
- ☐ **D**   Faith schools

QUESTION 4   Is the following statement ☐ TRUE or ☐ FALSE?

'The Prince of Wales is the head of the Church of Wales.'

QUESTION 5   Which statement is correct?

- ☐ **A**   The official report of the proceedings of Parliament is called Hansard.
- ☐ **B**   The official report of the proceedings of Parliament is called UK Parliamentary Proceedings.

QUESTION 6   Is the statement below   ☐ TRUE or ☐ FALSE?

'An employee can be dismissed immediately for serious misconduct at work.'

QUESTION 7   Children aged 13–16 cannot work for more than how many hours in a school week?

☐ **A**   10
☐ **B**   9
☐ **C**   12
☐ **D**   15

QUESTION 8   Which statement is correct?

☐ **A**   Prescriptions and treatment from a GP are free.
☐ **B**   Treatment from a GP is free but you have to pay a charge for prescriptions.

QUESTION 9   St George's Day in England is traditionally celebrated on

☐ **A**   23rd April
☐ **B**   30th November
☐ **C**   17th March
☐ **D**   25th December

QUESTION 10   A by-election is held

☐ **A**   half-way through the life of a Parliament
☐ **B**   every 2 years
☐ **C**   when an MP dies or resigns
☐ **D**   when the Prime Minister decides to call one

QUESTION 11   Jobcentre Plus is run by the

☐ **A**   Home Office
☐ **B**   local county council
☐ **C**   HM Revenue and Customs
☐ **D**   Department for Work and Pensions

QUESTION 12   Is the statement below   ☐ TRUE or ☐ FALSE?

'It is not usual for young people to have a part-time job while they are still at school.'

QUESTION 13   Is the statement below   ☐ TRUE or ☐ FALSE?

'Everything you tell a GP is private and confidential.'

QUESTION 14   In the late 19th and early 20th centuries, many women demonstrated for what right?

☐ **A**   The right to vote

☐ **B**   The right to equal pay

☐ **C**   The right to divorce their husbands

☐ **D**   The right to have an abortion

QUESTION 15   The Queen has reigned over the UK since her father's death in

☐ **A**   1945

☐ **B**   1958

☐ **C**   1952

☐ **D**   1951

QUESTION 16   Which TWO groups of people can take part in New Deal?

☐ **A**   Young people who have been unemployed for 6 months.

☐ **B**   Adults who have been unemployed for 12 months.

☐ **C**   Adults who have been unemployed for 18 months.

☐ **D**   Young people who have been unemployed for 8 months.

QUESTION 17   After the First World War, women got the right to vote and to be elected to parliament at the age of

☐ **A**   16

☐ **B**   18

☐ **C**   21

☐ **D**   30

QUESTION 18   Is the statement below   ☐ TRUE or ☐ FALSE?

'Independent secondary schools are sometimes called public schools.'

QUESTION 19 Large numbers of people from Eastern Europe have come to live in the UK since

☐ **A**   1987

☐ **B**   1992

☐ **C**   2001

☐ **D**   2004

QUESTION 20 In the UK, the legal voting age is

☐ **A**   16

☐ **B**   17

☐ **C**   18

☐ **D**   21

QUESTION 21 You can get information about training opportunities at which TWO places?

☐ **A**   Your local college

☐ **B**   Learndirect

☐ **C**   The Home Office

☐ **D**   The post office

QUESTION 22 In 2001 the population of the UK was nearly

☐ **A**   56 million

☐ **B**   58 million

☐ **C**   60 million

☐ **D**   62 million

QUESTION 23 Your employer should give you a written contract or statement with all the details and conditions for your work within

☐ **A**   6 months of starting the job

☐ **B**   4 months of starting the job

☐ **C**   3 months of starting the job

☐ **D**   2 months of starting the job

QUESTION 24   How many senior MPs make up the Cabinet?

☐ **A**   12

☐ **B**   15

☐ **C**   20

☐ **D**   10

Answers and pointers to questions in Practice Test 15

Question	Answer	Reference (page number in Life in the United Kingdom)	Notes
1	C	58	
2	A and D	35	
3	B and D	67	
4	False	39	There is no established church in Wales.
5	A	49	
6	True	81	
7	C	84	During school holidays, children aged 13–14 can work up to 25 hours per week, and children aged 15–16 can work up to 35 hours per week.
8	B	63	
9	A	39	
10	C	44	
11	D	75	
12	False	31	It is common for young people to have a part-time job while they are at school.
13	True	62	Information cannot be passed on without your permission.
14	A	29	
15	C	44	
16	A and C	82	
17	D	29	
18	True	67	
19	D	36	
20	C	49	
21	A and B	76	
22	C	35	
23	D	79	
24	C	45	

PRACTICE TEST 16

QUESTION 1   Is the statement below   ☐ TRUE or ☐ FALSE?

'If you have problems with your neighbours, you should contact the police for details of mediation organisations that can help solve disputes.'

QUESTION 2   Is the statement below   ☐ TRUE or ☐ FALSE?

'One-third of all Christians in the UK are Roman Catholic.'

QUESTION 3   School term dates are decided by

☐ **A**   the head teacher

☐ **B**   the parent/teachers' association

☐ **C**   the local education authority

☐ **D**   the National Union of Teachers

QUESTION 4   Which TWO of the following are public holidays in England?

☐ **A**   1st January

☐ **B**   2nd January

☐ **C**   31st October

☐ **D**   26th December

QUESTION 5   Where is the Prime Minister's official residence?

☐ **A**   Chequers

☐ **B**   10 Downing Street

☐ **C**   11 Downing Street

☐ **D**   Buckingham Palace

QUESTION 6   If you feel you have been unfairly dismissed from your job, you may be able to get compensation by taking your case to

☐ **A**   the local Magistrates' Court

☐ **B**   the Home Office

☐ **C**   an employment tribunal

☐ **D**   HM Revenue and Customs

QUESTION 7   Which of these statements is correct?

   ☐ **A** It is illegal to sell tobacco products to anyone under 21 years of age.

   ☐ **B** It is illegal to sell tobacco products to anyone under 18 years of age.

QUESTION 8   You must get insurance for which TWO?

   ☐ **A** A bicycle

   ☐ **B** A motorcycle

   ☐ **C** A car

   ☐ **D** A dog

QUESTION 9   Is the following statement   ☐ TRUE or ☐ FALSE?

   'There are twice as many Hindus as Jews in the UK.'

QUESTION 10   Debates in the House of Commons are chaired by

   ☐ **A** the Prime Minister

   ☐ **B** the Speaker

   ☐ **C** the monarch

   ☐ **D** the leader of the Opposition

QUESTION 11   Is the statement below   ☐ TRUE or ☐ FALSE?

   'Everyone in the UK has the right to work.'

QUESTION 12   The percentage of children who live in a stepfamily is

   ☐ **A** 10

   ☐ **B** 15

   ☐ **C** 20

   ☐ **D** 25

QUESTION 13   Which statement is correct?

- ☐ **A**   If you want to see a doctor, you should ask your pharmacist for an appointment.
- ☐ **B**   If you want to see a doctor, you should make an appointment at your local health centre.

QUESTION 14   What percentage of the UK workforce are women?

- ☐ **A**   43%
- ☐ **B**   45%
- ☐ **C**   49%
- ☐ **D**   51%

QUESTION 15   Is the statement below   ☐ TRUE or ☐ FALSE?

'Convicted prisoners can vote.'

QUESTION 16   Which statement is correct?

- ☐ **A**   The ChildcareLink website gives information about different kinds of childcare in your area.
- ☐ **B**   The Childline website gives information about different kinds of childcare in your area.

QUESTION 17   Is the statement below   ☐ TRUE or ☐ FALSE?

'In the UK, most children get pocket money from their parents.'

QUESTION 18   In England and Wales, Skills for Life courses include which TWO subjects?

- ☐ **A**   Woodwork
- ☐ **B**   Literacy
- ☐ **C**   Plumbing
- ☐ **D**   Numeracy

QUESTION 19 Which of these statements is correct?

☐ **A** The population of Wales is nearly 3 million.

☐ **B** The population of Wales is nearly 5 million.

QUESTION 20 Which statement is correct?

☐ **A** To become a local councillor you must have a local connection with the area.

☐ **B** To become a local councillor you must be from the area.

QUESTION 21 How long does a father have to work for his employer before he is entitled to paternity leave?

☐ **A** 26 weeks

☐ **B** 1 year

☐ **C** 2 years

☐ **D** 12 weeks

QUESTION 22 Which TWO of the following statistics does the census collect?

☐ **A** Age

☐ **B** Height

☐ **C** Weight

☐ **D** Occupation

QUESTION 23 Which of these statements is correct?

☐ **A** Most employees who are aged 16 or over are entitled to at least 5 weeks' paid holiday every year.

☐ **B** Most employees who are aged 16 or over are entitled to at least 4 weeks' paid holiday every year.

QUESTION 24   Which of the following statements is correct?

☐ **A**   Anyone can stand for election to the UK Parliament.

☐ **B**   Only those who have been nominated to represent a political party can stand for election to the UK Parliament.

Answers and pointers to questions in Practice Test 16

Question	Answer	Reference (page number in Life in the United Kingdom)	Notes
1	False	59	You can get details of mediation organisations from your local authority, the Citizens' Advice Bureau and Mediation UK.
2	False	38	10% of all Christians in the UK are Roman Catholic.
3	C	68	
4	A and D	40	1st January is a public holiday in the whole of the UK. 2nd January is a public holiday only in Scotland.
5	B	45	
6	C	81	
7	B	31	
8	B and C	61	
9	True	38	1% of the population is Hindu and 0.5% of the population is Jewish.
10	B	46	
11	False	75	
12	A	30	
13	B	63	
14	B	29	
15	False	49	
16	A	84	
17	True	30	
18	B and D	68	
19	A	35	The population of Wales is 2.9 million (5% of the UK population).
20	A	50	
21	A	84	

Question	Answer	Reference (page number in Life in the United Kingdom)	Notes
22	A and D	35	
23	B	79	
24	A	46	

PRACTICE TEST 17

QUESTION 1   What insurance is compulsory for the following items?

☐ **A**   Credit cards

☐ **B**   Health

☐ **C**   Car or motorcycle

☐ **D**   Mobile phones

QUESTION 2   The percentage of the UK population who live in Scotland is

☐ **A**   5%

☐ **B**   8%

☐ **C**   15%

☐ **D**   20%

QUESTION 3   Is the statement below   ☐ TRUE or ☐ FALSE?

'Parents are excluded from membership of a school's governing body which decides how the school is run and administered.'

QUESTION 4   The head of the Church of England is

☐ **A**   the Archbishop of Canterbury

☐ **B**   the Prime Minister

☐ **C**   the Queen

☐ **D**   the Moderator

QUESTION 5   Who has the task of applying the Human Rights Act?

☐ **A**   The House of Commons

☐ **B**   The police

☐ **C**   The House of Lords

☐ **D**   The judiciary

QUESTION 6   Which of these statements is correct?

☐ **A**   If you lose your job because the company you work for no longer needs you, you may be entitled to an extra payment.

☐ **B**   If you lose your job because the company you work for no longer needs you, you will not be entitled to any extra payment.

QUESTION 7   Is the statement below   ☐ TRUE or ☐ FALSE?

'There are more women than men in Britain.'

QUESTION 8   Is the statement below   ☐ TRUE or ☐ FALSE?

'Scotland and Wales have their own banknotes which are valid everywhere in the UK.'

QUESTION 9   Which of the following statements is true?

☐ **A**   45% of all ethnic minority people in the UK live in London.

☐ **B**   35% of all ethnic minority people in the UK live in London.

QUESTION 10   The Scottish Parliament meets at

☐ **A**   Holyrood

☐ **B**   Holywood

☐ **C**   Holywell

☐ **D**   Holyhead

QUESTION 11   When you apply for a job, you often need to send which TWO things?

☐ **A**   A signed photograph

☐ **B**   A curriculum vitae

☐ **C**   A National Insurance number

☐ **D**   A covering letter

QUESTION 12   Children must go to school between the ages of

☐ **A**   4 and 16

☐ **B**   5 and 16

☐ **C**   6 and 16

☐ **D**   5 and 18

QUESTION 13   Is the statement below   ☐ TRUE or ☐ FALSE?

'Education at state schools is free but parents have to pay for school uniform and sports wear.'

QUESTION 14   Is the statement below   ☐ TRUE or ☐ FALSE?

'There are 2 million children at work in the UK at any one time.'

QUESTION 15   A by-election happens in a constituency when which TWO of the following events happen?

☐ **A**   The MP dies

☐ **B**   The Lord Chancellor decides

☐ **C**   The Prime Minister decides

☐ **D**   The MP resigns

QUESTION 16   Is the statement below   ☐ TRUE or ☐ FALSE?

'British citizens can work in any country that is a member of the European Economic Area.'

QUESTION 17   In the late 1960s and early 1970s, the government restricted immigration to the UK. Which TWO countries did not face these controls?

☐ **A**   Canada

☐ **B**   France

☐ **C**   South Africa

☐ **D**   Australia

QUESTION 18   Is the statement below   ☐ TRUE or ☐ FALSE?

*'If you do not have an MOT certificate, and your car is more than
3 years old, your car insurance will not be valid.'*

QUESTION 19   The TWO main Christian festivals are

☐ **A**   Diwali

☐ **B**   Christmas

☐ **C**   New Year

☐ **D**   Easter

QUESTION 20   Members of the European Parliament (MEPs) are elected every

☐ **A**   year

☐ **B**   2 years

☐ **C**   5 years

☐ **D**   10 years

QUESTION 21   Which TWO of the following statements is correct?

An employee can be dismissed from their job if

☐ **A**   they cannot do their job properly

☐ **B**   they are pregnant

☐ **C**   they are unacceptably late

☐ **D**   they have a disability

QUESTION 22   Is the following statement   ☐ TRUE or ☐ FALSE?

'There are more children aged under 16 in Britain than people over 60.'

QUESTION 23   National Insurance (NI) contributions are used to help pay for which TWO of the following benefits?

☐ **A**   State libraries
☐ **B**   National Health Service
☐ **C**   Universities
☐ **D**   State retirement pension

QUESTION 24   Is the following statement   ☐ TRUE or ☐ FALSE?

'In the UK, a judge decides whether someone is guilty or innocent of a serious crime.'

Answers and pointers to questions in Practice Test 17

Question	Answer	Reference (page number in Life in the United Kingdom)	Notes
1	C	61	
2	B	35	5.1 million people live in Scotland – that is, 8% of the UK population.
3	False	68	A number of places on school governing bodies are reserved for parents.
4	C	39	The King or Queen is the head, or Supreme Governor, of the Church of England.
5	D	48	
6	A	81	
7	True	29	Women make up 51% of the population.
8	False	60	Northern Ireland and Scotland have their own banknotes which are valid everywhere in the UK.
9	A	37	
10	A	51	
11	B and D	76	
12	B	30	
13	True	66	
14	True	31	It is common for young people to have a part-time job while they are still at school.
15	A and D	44	
16	True	82	
17	A and D	28	
18	True	72	
19	B and D	40	
20	C	53	
21	A and C	81	

Question	Answer	Reference (page number in Life in the United Kingdom)	Notes
22	False	35	
23	B and D	80	
24	False	48	Judges cannot decide whether people are guilty or innocent of a serious crime. When someone is accused of a serious crime, a jury decides whether he or she is innocent or guilty, and if guilty the judge will decide on the penalty.

RELATED PUBLICATIONS

TSO (The Stationery Office)

TSO publishes the official Home Office guide *Life in the United Kingdom: A Journey to Citizenship* plus *Life in the UK: Official Citizenship Test Study Guide.*

You can buy these publications from all good high street bookstores or direct from TSO by visiting www.tsoshop.co.uk/LIUK or calling 0870 243 0123.

Life in the United Kingdom : A Journey to Citizenship is available in the following formats:

Life in the United Kingdom: A Journey to Citizenship
2nd Edition (2007)   Book   ISBN 9780113413133   £9.99

Life in the United Kingdom: A Journey to Citizenship
2nd Edition (2007)   Downloadable PDF   ISBN 9780113413232   £9.99 (£11.49 inc. VAT)

Life in the United Kingdom: A Journey to Citizenship
2nd Edition (2007)   Large Print   ISBN 9780113413171   £9.99

Life in the United Kingdom: A Journey to Citizenship
2nd Edition (2007)   Audio CD   ISBN 9780113413188   £9.99 (£11.49 inc. VAT)

Life in the United Kingdom: Official Citizenship Test Study Guide is available in the following formats:

Life in the United Kingdom: Official Citizenship Test Study Guide
1st Edition (2008)   Book   ISBN 9780113413249   £5.99

Life in the United Kingdom: Official Citizenship Test Study Guide
1st Edition (2008)   Downloadable PDF   ISBN 9780113413140   £5.99 (£6.89 inc. VAT)

Don't forget to practise the Life in the UK test online at www.tsoshop.co.uk/TEST.

Prepare to pass first time with the official publications.